# just eggs

**Published by:**
TRIDENT REFERENCE PUBLISHING
801 12th Avenue South, Suite 400
Naples, Fl 34102 USA

Tel: + 1 (239) 649-7077
www.tridentreference.com
email: sales@tridentreference.com

# just eggs

Just Eggs
© TRIDENT REFERENCE PUBLISHING

**Publisher**
Simon St. John Bailey

**Editor-in-chief**
Susan Knightley

**Prepress**
Precision Prep & Press

Includes Index
ISBN 1582796750
UPC 6 15269 96750 8

Printed in The United States

# introduction

We have all heard the saying "If there is an egg in the house there is a meal in the house". Eggs are one of nature's fast foods –it takes only minutes to whisk up and cook an omelette or to create delicious crêpes. For something that's sure to impress, an aired soufflé –whether it's sweet or savory– must be your choice everytime.

# just eggs
## introduction

This book presents a wonderful collection of dishes that use eggs as their main ingredient. You will find recipes for imaginative brunches, inspiring main meals and tempting desserts.

### What's in an egg?

- About 75% of an egg is water, 12% is protein and 12% is fat. An egg weighing 60 g/2 oz with its shell on supplies approximately 6 g protein, 6 g fat, a trace of sugars and starch, no dietary fiber and 85 calories.

- Eggs also contain good amounts of calcium, phosphorus, potassium, zinc and iron –however it should be remembered that the iron in eggs is not well absorbed by humans. They are also good sources of the B group vitamins, plus vitamins A, D and E.

- In recent years there has been much publicity about the amount of cholesterol contained in eggs and while one egg contains about 250 mg cholesterol, this should not stop you from including them as a part of a balanced diet. If you have high blood cholesterol it is advised that you should limit your egg intake to two per week.

## Buying and storing eggs

- Always buy eggs from a reliable source with a high turnover to ensure you are getting the freshest possible eggs.

- In some countries in recent years there has been concern over the levels of salmonella bacteria in eggs. Any risks can be eliminated by making sure that eggs are well cooked. When making mayonnaise, the addition of vinegar or lemon juice will kill any bacteria. In meringues the high proportion of sugar prevents problems.

- Eggs should be stored in the refrigerator with the pointed egg down –this helps keep the yolk centered. Keeping the eggs in their carton protects them from odors. The shell of an egg is porous, so if stored with strong-smelling foods, such as onions, the eggs can absorb and take on that flavor.

## Difficulty scale

■□□ I Easy to do

■■□ I Requires attention

■■■ I Requires experience

# tossed
## egg salad

■☐☐ | Cooking time: 10 minutes - Preparation time: 5 minutes

## method

1. Tightly pack eggs into a saucepan, pointed end down (a), cover with water and bring to the boil. Boil for 10 minutes. Drain eggs and cool under cold running water.
   Peel eggs as soon as they are cool (b).
   Cut in halves (c) or slices.
2. Arrange lettuce, green and black olives, eggs, red pepper and celery on a large platter.
3. To make dressing, place vinegar, honey, lime juice and oil in a screwtop jar and shake well to combine. Drizzle over salad and serve immediately.

...............................
**Serves 4 as a light meal**

## ingredients

> **4 eggs**
> **1 lettuce, leaves separated**
> **10 stuffed green olives, halved**
> **5 black olives, stoned and sliced**
> **1 red pepper, cut into thin strips**
> **2 stalks celery, cut into thin strips**

### honey dressing

> **2 tablespoons red wine vinegar**
> **1 teaspoon honey**
> **1 tablespoon lime juice**
> **1 teaspoon olive oil**

## tip from the chef

*Ideal for weight watchers, this salad is an elegant lunch or supper dish. For a complete meal, accompany with crusty bread and finish with a piece of fresh fruit.*

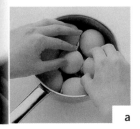

a

b

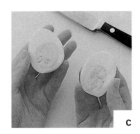

c

# scotch eggs

■□□ I Cooking time: 5 minutes - Preparation time: 5 minutes

## ingredients

> **4 hard-boiled eggs**
> **500 g/1 lb sausage mince**
> **1 egg, lightly beaten**
> **pinch cayenne pepper**
> **1 cup dried breadcrumbs**
> **oil for deep-frying**

## method

1. Carefully shell eggs. Divide sausage mince into 4 rounds, pat out each round with damp hands. Place one egg on each circle (a) and shape it carefully around the egg so that the egg is completely enclosed.
2. Roll in combined beaten egg and cayenne pepper, then in breadcrumbs (b).
3. Heat oil in a saucepan over moderate heat, deep-fry eggs (c) until golden brown and cooked through.

............

**Serves 4**

tip from the chef

*Quick cooling of hard-boiled eggs prevents a dark ring forming around the yolk.*

a

b

c

# quail egg salad

■□□ | Cooking time: 6 minutes - Preparation time: 5 minutes

## method

1. Bring a large saucepan of water to the boil, add quails' eggs and cook for 3 minutes. Drain and set aside to cool. Shell eggs and reserve.
2. Heat oil in a large frying pan over a medium heat and cook garlic and leeks for 3 minutes or until tender. Arrange radicchio leaves or red cabbage on plates, top with warm leek mixture and 3 eggs.
3. To make dressing, place garlic, oil, lemon juice and black pepper to taste in a screwtop jar and shake to combine. Sprinkle over salads and serve immediately.

...........

**Serves 4**

## ingredients

> **12 quails' eggs**
> **1 tablespoon olive oil**
> **2 cloves garlic, crushed**
> **2 leeks, cut into thin strips**
> **1 radicchio, leaves separated, or $1/4$ red cabbage, shredded**

### french dressing

> **1 clove garlic, crushed**
> **2 tablespoons olive oil**
> **3 tablespoons lemon juice**
> **freshly ground black pepper**

## tip from the chef

*If quails' eggs are unavailable, this salad is just as delicious made with hens' eggs. Use 3 hens' eggs, hard-boiled and cut into quarters, in place of the quails' eggs.*

# coconut
## curried eggs

■□□ | Cooking time: 25 minutes - Preparation time: 10 minutes

## ingredients
> **8 hard-boiled eggs**
> **30 g/1 oz butter**
> **1 onion, chopped**
> **2 teaspoons curry powder**
> **1 teaspoon ground cumin**
> **1 tablespoon cornflour**
> **1 cup chicken stock**
> **1 cup coconut milk**
> **2 tablespoons lemon juice**

## method
1. Peel and halve eggs, place into a greased 8-cups capacity ovenproof dish.
2. Melt butter in a saucepan, add onion, stir-fry until tender. Add curry and cumin, stir over heat 1 minute.
3. Pour in combined cornflour, stock, coconut milk and lemon juice, stir until mixture boils and thickens.
4. Pour curry sauce over eggs, cover, bake in moderate oven for 20 minutes or until heated through.

...........
**Serves 4**

tip from the chef
*Serve with boiled rice, if desired.*

# egg
## and avocado tomatoes

■□□ I Cooking time: 5 minutes - Preparation time: 5 minutes

## method

1. Cut tops from tomatoes and scoop out seeds and flesh to make tomato shells.
2. Place eggs, chives, avocado and black pepper to taste in a bowl and mix to combine. Melt butter in a frying pan over a low heat, add egg mixture and cook, stirring gently, until set but still creamy.
3. Divide egg mixture between tomato shells and top each filled tomato with a teaspoon of sour cream or yogurt.

Serves 4

## ingredients

> 4 large tomatoes
> 4 eggs, lightly beaten
> 1 tablespoon snipped fresh chives
> 1/4 avocado, peeled and chopped
> freshly ground black pepper
> 60 g/2 oz butter
> 4 teaspoons sour cream or natural yogurt

## tip from the chef

*A wonderful combination of flavors, these tomatoes are just right for that special breakfast, brunch or supper.*

# pipérade
## with eggs

■□□ | Cooking time: 15 minutes - Preparation time: 10 minutes

## ingredients

> **8 eggs**
> **¹/2 cup/125 ml/4 fl oz orange juice**
> **¹/3 cup/90 ml/3 fl oz double cream**
> **30 g/1 oz butter**

### pipérade

> **30 g/1 oz butter**
> **1 small leek, sliced**
> **250 g/8 oz ham, diced**
> **1 teaspoon dried oregano**
> **1 green pepper, chopped**
> **1 yellow or red pepper, chopped**
> **125 g/4 oz cherry tomatoes, halved**
> **freshly ground black pepper**

## method

1. To make pipérade, melt butter in a frying pan and cook leek, ham, oregano, green and yellow or red peppers for 4-5 minutes or until leek and peppers are soft. Add tomatoes and cook for 2-3 minutes or until heated. Season to taste with black pepper. Set aside and keep warm.

2. Place eggs, orange juice, cream and black pepper to taste in a bowl and mix to combine. Melt butter in a frying pan, add egg mixture and cook over a low heat. As the egg mixture starts to set, gently turn it, so that the mixture forms large fluffy rolls –do not use a stirring motion as this causes the rolls to break up. Cook until all the egg mixture is just set.

3. Spoon egg around the outside of a large serving platter, then spoon pipérade into the center.

...........

**Serves 8**

## tip from the chef

*Served with hot toast this is a substantial breakfast or brunch dish. It makes an excellent lunch or dinner dish.*

# ranch-style eggs

■□□ | Cooking time: 25 minutes - Preparation time: 10 minutes

## method

1. Melt butter in a heavy-based frying pan over a medium heat, add onion and cook, stirring, for 3-4 minutes or until soft, but not brown. Stir in tomatoes, chili and tomato paste, bring to simmering and simmer, stirring occasionally, for 10 minutes.

2. Using the back of a large spoon, make 4 hollows in the tomato mixture. Break an egg into a cup, then carefully slide into one of the hollows. Repeat with remaining eggs. Cover pan and cook for 5 minutes or until egg whites are just set.

3. Season eggs with black pepper and sprinkle with cheese. Re-cover pan and cook for 2 minutes longer or until cheese melts and eggs are cooked to your liking. Sprinkle with coriander and serve immediately.

## ingredients

> 30 g/1 oz butter
> 1 small onion, thinly sliced
> 440 g/14 oz canned tomatoes, drained and mashed
> 1 fresh green chili, seeded and cut into thin strips
> 2 tablespoons tomato paste (purée)
> 4 eggs
> freshly ground black pepper
> 125 g/4 oz tasty cheese (mature Cheddar), grated
> 2 tablespoons chopped fresh coriander

...........

**Serves 4**

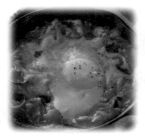

## tip from the chef

*For the best results use a well-seasoned cast iron frying pan when making this dish.*

# mushrooms
## filled with eggs

■□□ | Cooking time: 20 minutes - Preparation time: 10 minutes

## method

1. Melt butter in a frying pan and cook mushrooms over a medium heat, skin side down, for 1 minute. Remove mushrooms from pan and place in a lightly greased ovenproof dish.

2. Add onion, red pepper and garlic to pan and cook, stirring, for 5 minutes or until soft. Divide onion mixture between mushrooms.

3. Using the back of a spoon, make a depression in the mixture to form a nest. Break an egg into each mushroom. Top each egg with 1 tablespoon cream and sprinkle with 1 tablespoon cheese.

4. Bake at 180°C/350°F/Gas 4 for 10-15 minutes or until egg whites are set and cheese is melted.

### ingredients

> **30 g/1 oz butter**
> **4 large mushrooms, stalks removed**
> **1 onion, finely chopped**
> **1/2 red pepper, finely chopped**
> **1 clove garlic, crushed**
> **4 small eggs**
> **4 tablespoons cream**
> **4 tablespoons grated Gruyère cheese**

..........
**Serves 4**

tip from the chef

*In case the egg is bad, always break it into a separate glass or container before adding to the main mixture.*

# cheesy baked eggs

■□□ | Cooking time: 20 minutes - Preparation time: 10 minutes

## method

1. Melt butter in a frying pan and cook mushrooms and lettuce, stirring, for 4-5 minutes or until mushrooms are tender. Stir in Worcestershire sauce and season to taste with black pepper. Divide mushroom mixture between four-1 cup/ 250 ml/8 fl oz capacity ovenproof ramekins.

2. Break an egg into each ramekin and sprinkle with cheese. Bake at 200°C/400°F/Gas 6 for 10-15 minutes or until eggs are cooked and cheese is melted.

## ingredients

> **30 g/1 oz butter**
> **250 g/8 oz mushrooms, chopped**
> **1 lettuce, shredded**
> **1 tablespoon Worcestershire sauce**
> **freshly ground black pepper**
> **4 eggs**
> **60 g/2 oz tasty cheese (mature Cheddar), grated**

...........
**Serves 4**

## tip from the chef

*The fresher the egg the higher its food value. When a fresh egg is placed into a glass of water it will sink straight to the bottom. The yolk of a fresh egg sits in the middle of the egg white when broken onto a saucer.*

# provençal eggs

■☐☐ I Cooking time: 45 minutes - Preparation time: 10 minutes

## ingredients
> ¹/₂ cup/125 ml/4 fl oz vegetable oil
> 1 large onion, chopped
> 2 cloves garlic, crushed
> 1 eggplant, chopped
> 4 large tomatoes, chopped
> 3 tablespoons tomato paste (purée)
> ¹/₄ cup/60 ml/2 fl oz white wine
> 4 eggs
> 1 tablespoon chopped fresh parsley

## method
1. Heat 2 tablespoons oil in a large frying pan and cook onion and garlic for 3-4 minutes or until soft. Add eggplant and remaining oil and cook for 5 minutes. Stir in tomatoes, tomato paste and wine (a) and cook for 10 minutes longer.
2. Transfer vegetable mixture to a shallow ovenproof dish and bake at 200°C/400°F/Gas 6 for 10 minutes.
3. Remove dish from oven and using the back of a tablespoon make 4 depressions in the mixture (b). Break an egg into each depression (c), sprinkle with parsley and bake for 10-15 minutes longer or until eggs are cooked.

...........
**Serves 4**

## tip from the chef
*This delightful dish can also be cooked in shallow individual dishes. Divide vegetable mixture between dishes, bake for 5 minutes then add the eggs and bake for 10 minutes longer or until eggs are cooked.*

a

b

c

# egg and mustard ham rolls

■☐☐ I Cooking time: 30 minutes - Preparation time: 15 minutes

## method

1. Cut a slice from the top of each bread roll; set aside and reserve. Scoop out the center, leaving a thin shell (reserve crumbs for another use). Spread inside of each roll with mustard.

2. Melt butter in a frying pan over a medium heat and cook mushrooms and onion for 2-3 minutes. Add ham and cook for 2 minutes longer. Divide mixture between rolls and sprinkle with black pepper.

3. Break an egg into a small bowl, then slide it into a roll. Repeat with remaining eggs and rolls. Sprinkle with cheese and replace the tops.

4. Place rolls on a baking tray and bake at 180°C/350°F/Gas 4 for 25 minutes or until whites are firm.

## ingredients

> **4 wholemeal rolls**
> **2 tablespoons wholegrain mustard**
> **15 g/1/2 oz butter**
> **50 g/13/4 oz button mushrooms, sliced**
> **1 onion, chopped**
> **50 g/13/4 oz thin ham slices, cut into strips**
> **freshly ground black pepper**
> **4 eggs**
> **60 g/2 oz Cheddar cheese, grated**

...........

**Serves 4**

## tip from the chef

*These rolls make a great snack or a delicious brunch. For a quick and nutritious meal, serve with a tossed green salad.*

# homemade
## mayonnaise

■ ■ □ | Cooking time: 0 minute - Preparation time: 10 minutes

## method

1. Place egg yolks, salt and mustard in a bowl. Beat vigorously with a wooden spoon until thickened. Add 60 ml/2 fl oz oil, drop by drop. Stir in half the vinegar or lemon juice.

2. Gradually add remaining oil in a thin stream, beating constantly. Stir in the remaining vinegar or lemon juice and season to taste with black pepper.
If too thin, add 1-2 tablespoons hot water, beating well.

3. Pour mayonnaise into a sterilized jar. Cover and store in the refrigerator for 1-2 weeks.

### ingredients

> **2 egg yolks**
> **1/2 teaspoon salt**
> **1 teaspoon Dijon mustard**
> **300 ml/10 fl oz olive oil**
> **2 teaspoons vinegar or lemon juice**
> **freshly ground black pepper**

....................................
**Makes about 365 ml/12 fl oz**

tip from the chef
*To make mayonnaise using a food processor, use 1 whole egg instead of 2 egg yolks and make in the same way, adding the oil in a slow steady stream with the motor running.*

# asparagus
## with orange hollandaise

■□□ | Cooking time: 5 minutes - Preparation time: 5 minutes

## method

1. Bring a large saucepan of water to the boil. Add asparagus and simmer for 2 minutes or until just tender, drain.
2. Combine egg yolks, lemon juice, orange juice and orange rind in a blender or food processor, blend for 10 seconds.
3. Melt butter in a small saucepan until bubbling, immediately pour into food processor or blender, while motor is operating, in a slow steady stream.
4. Place asparagus on a serving plate, spoon sauce over the top and garnish with strips of orange rind.

### ingredients

> **2 bunches fresh asparagus, trimmed**
> **3 egg yolks**
> **1 tablespoon freshly squeezed lemon juice**
> **1 tablespoon freshly squeezed orange juice**
> **3 teaspoons finely grated orange rind**
> **125 g/4 oz butter**

...........
**Serves 4**

### tip from the chef

*It is best to bring eggs to room temperature before using. Remove the eggs from the refrigerator 30 minutes before use or run them under warm water for a short time. Eggs at room temperature cook more evenly and if you are beating them they will have an increased volume.*

# open
## béarnaise burgers

■□□ | Cooking time: 15 minutes - Preparation time: 10 minutes

## method

1. To make patties, place beef mince, lemon rind, onion, garlic, tarragon, egg and bread crumbs in a bowl and mix to combine. Divide mixture into twelve and shape into small patties. Cook patties under a preheated grill for 4-5 minutes each side or until cooked to your liking. Remove from grill, drain on absorbent kitchen paper and keep warm.

2. To make sauce, place egg yolks, tarragon, vinegar and lemon juice in a food processor or blender and process until smooth. Melt butter until it is hot and bubbling. With machine running, slowly pour in melted butter and process until sauce is thick.

3. To assemble, split and toast muffins. Top each muffin half with a lettuce leaf, three patties and a little sauce. Serve immediately.

...........
Serves 4

## ingredients

> 2 English muffins
> 4 lettuce leaves

### beef patties

> 500 g/1 lb lean beef mince
> 1 teaspoon finely grated lemon rind
> 1 small onion, finely chopped
> 1 clove garlic, crushed
> 3 teaspoons finely chopped fresh tarragon or 1 teaspoon dried tarragon
> 1 egg
> 1/4 cup/30 g/1 oz dried bread crumbs

### béarnaise sauce

> 3 egg yolks
> 3 teaspoons finely chopped fresh tarragon or 1 teaspoon dried tarragon
> 1 tablespoon tarragon vinegar
> 1 tablespoon lemon juice
> 250 g/8 oz butter

## tip from the chef

*These sophisticated mini burgers are sure to be popular with everyone who likes good food.*

# bacon
## and herb omelettes

■□□ I Cooking time: 10 minutes - Preparation time: 10 minutes

## ingredients

> **2 teaspoons vegetable oil**
> **2 leeks, chopped**
> **6 rashers bacon, chopped**
> **2 tablespoons chopped fresh parsley**
> **2 tablespoons chopped fresh basil**
> **2 tablespoons chopped fresh oregano**
> **6 eggs, lightly beaten**
> **1/2 cup/125 ml/4 fl oz milk**
> **60 g/2 oz tasty cheese (mature Cheddar), grated**
> **freshly ground black pepper**
> **4 thick slices wholemeal bread, toasted**

## method

1. Heat oil in a wok over a medium heat, add leeks and bacon and stir-fry for 5 minutes or until bacon is crisp. Transfer to a bowl, add parsley, basil and oregano and mix to combine. Set aside.

2. Place eggs, milk, cheese and black pepper to taste in a bowl and whisk to combine. Pour 1/4 of the egg mixture into wok and swirl so mixture covers base and sides. Top with 1/4 of the leek mixture and cook for 1 minute or until set.

3. Remove from wok, roll up and place on a slice of toast. Repeat with remaining mixture to make 4 omelettes.

...........
**Serves 4**

### tip from the chef

*Fresh mint can be used in place of oregano if you wish. For a vegetarian version omit bacon and replace with well-drained cooked spinach. Squeeze as much moisture as possible from the spinach before making the omelette.*

# spring omelette

a

■□□ | Cooking time: 5 minutes - Preparation time: 5 minutes

## method

1. To make filling, melt butter in a frying pan and cook spring onions, mushrooms, red pepper and coriander for 2 minutes or until tender. Remove from pan, set aside and keep warm.
2. Melt butter in a clean omelette pan. Place eggs, milk and black pepper to taste in a bowl and whisk to combine (a). Pour half the egg mixture into pan and, as the omelette cooks, use a palette knife, fork or skewer to gently draw up the edge of the omelette (b) until no liquid remains and the omelette is lightly set.
3. Top half the omelette with half the filling, then sprinkle with half the cheese. Fold omelette over, slide onto a serving plate (c). Repeat with remaining ingredients and serve immediately.

...........
**Serves 2**

## ingredients

> **15 g/¹/2 oz butter**
> **4 eggs, lightly beaten**
> **3 tablespoons milk**
> **freshly ground black pepper**
> **3 tablespoons grated tasty cheese (mature Cheddar)**

### vegetable filling

> **15 g/¹/2 oz butter**
> **2 spring onions, finely chopped**
> **6 button mushrooms, sliced**
> **¹/2 small red pepper, cut into thin strips**
> **1 teaspoon chopped fresh coriander**

### tip from the chef

*If you do not have a special omelette pan, use an aluminum frying pan. Prepare the frying pan by rubbing with a small amount of salt and kitchen paper. Remove all traces of salt before cooking. You can also use a nonstick frying pan. However if you intend making omelettes on a regular basis it is well worth investing in a good pan.*

b

c

# pickled
## vegetable omelette

■□□ | Cooking time: 15 minutes - Preparation time: 5 minutes

## ingredients
> **2 tablespoons peanut oil**
> **250 g/8 oz lean beef mince**
> **2 tablespoons Chinese pickled vegetables (tung chai), drained and chopped**
> **1 teaspoon honey**
> **2 tablespoons soy sauce**
> **6 spring onions, finely chopped**
> **6 eggs, lightly beaten**

## method
1. Heat 1 tablespoon oil in a frying pan and stir-fry beef mince, vegetables, honey, soy sauce and spring onions for 3-4 minutes or until cooked. Remove from pan, set aside and keep warm.
2. Heat remaining oil in a clean frying pan, pour in 1/4 of the beaten eggs. Swirl pan to make a thin omelette. Spoon 1/4 of the meat mixture into the center of the omelette and fold over the edges.
3. Remove omelette from pan, set aside and keep warm. Repeat with remaining eggs and meat mixture. Cut omelettes into slices and serve immediately.

...........

**Serves 4**

tip from the chef
*The Chinese mixed vegetables used as the filling for this omelette are available from most Oriental supermarkets.*

# cream cheese
## and ricotta crêpes

■□□ | Cooking time: 5 minutes - Preparation time: 10 minutes

## method

1. Sift flour into a medium bowl, gradually stir in the combined eggs and milk, stir until smooth. Pour mixture through a sieve to remove any lumps.
2. Heat a medium frying pan over moderate heat, grease lightly and pour about 4 tablespoons of batter into frying pan. Tilt pan so batter covers base thinly and evenly (a). Cook until lightly browned on base; turn crêpe, using a palette knife (b), and cook second side. Remove from pan and repeat with remaining mixture.
3. To make filling, blend or process cream cheese with ricotta, chives and nutmeg until quite smooth. Stir in Parmesan cheese, corn and parsley.
4. Place about 3 tablespoons of mixture onto each crêpe and roll up.

## ingredients

> 1 cup plain flour
> 3 eggs, lightly beaten
> 1 cup milk
> butter for greasing
> 125 g/4 oz cream cheese
> 250 g/$^{1}/_{2}$ lb ricotta cheese
> 3 tablespoons chopped fresh chives
> $^{1}/_{2}$ teaspoon ground nutmeg
> $^{1}/_{4}$ cup freshly grated Parmesan cheese
> $^{1}/_{2}$ cup canned sweet corn kernels, drained
> 2 tablespoons finely chopped fresh parsley

..........
Serves 4

a

b

## tip from the chef

*To freeze crêpes without filling, stack them between sheets of freezer wrap, place in a freezer bag and seal. To use crêpes, thaw at room temperature, then fill.*

# herb
## and parmesan soufflé

■□□ | Cooking time: 35 minutes - Preparation time: 10 minutes

## ingredients
> **50 g/1³/4 oz butter**
> **3 tablespoons plain flour**
> **300 ml/10 fl oz milk**
> **155 g/5 oz mature Cheddar cheese, grated**
> **75 g/2¹/2 oz Parmesan cheese, grated**
> **¹/4 teaspoon ground nutmeg**
> **1 cup chopped fresh herbs**
> **4 eggs, separated**

## method
1. Melt butter in a large saucepan over moderate heat. Add flour, cook for 1 minute, slowly add milk (a) and stir constantly until sauce is thick and smooth.
2. Stir in Cheddar cheese, Parmesan cheese, nutmeg, herbs and seasoning to taste, mix well, then beat in egg yolks one at a time (b).
3. Beat egg whites until soft peaks form, fold into cheese mixture (c), half a cup at a time.
4. Pour mixture into a greased 4-cup capacity soufflé dish and bake in a moderate oven for 25-30 minutes.

..........
**Serves 4**

### tip from the chef
*When folding egg whites into a mixture, first mix in 2-3 tablespoons of the egg whites to loosen the mixture. Then add the remaining egg whites and gently fold them in, using a spatula.*

a

b

c

# onion quiches

■□□ | Cooking time: 25 minutes - Preparation time: 5 minutes

## method

1. Line 6 individual flan tins with pastry. Melt butter in a frying pan and cook onions until golden. Divide into pastry cases.
2. Combine eggs, sour cream and nutmeg. Pour into quiches. Top with cheese and bake at 220°C/400°F/Gas 6 for 20 minutes or until firm.

### ingredients

> **3 sheets puff pastry**
> **60 g/2 oz butter**
> **4 onions, sliced**
> **4 eggs, beaten**
> **1 3/4 cup/435 g/14 1/2 oz sour cream**
> **1 teaspoon ground nutmeg**
> **1 1/2 cup/180 g/6 oz grated tasty cheese**

..........

**Serves 6**

### tip from the chef

*If you wish, add 1 teaspoon dried dill leaves or 1/4 teaspoon ground dried dill along with nutmeg.*

# spinach roulade

a     b     c

■□□ | Cooking time: 15 minutes - Preparation time: 10 minutes

## method

1. Place spinach, flour, egg yolks, butter, nutmeg and black pepper to taste in a food processor or blender and process until combined. Transfer to a bowl.

2. Place egg whites in a bowl and beat until stiff peaks form, then mix 2 tablespoons of egg whites into spinach mixture (a). Fold remaining egg whites into spinach mixture. Spoon into a greased and lined 25 x 30 cm/10 x 12 in Swiss roll tin (b) and bake at 200°C/400°F/Gas 6 for 12 minutes or until firm.

3. To make filling, melt butter in a frying pan and cook mushrooms over a medium heat for 1 minute. Add spring onions, tomatoes, oregano, basil and black pepper to taste, and cook for 3 minutes longer.

4. Turn roulade onto a tea-towel, sprinkle with Parmesan cheese and roll up. Allow to stand for 1 minute. Unroll and spread with filling. Reroll (c) and serve immediately.

...........
**Serves 6**

## ingredients

> **250 g/8 oz frozen spinach, thawed**
> **1 tablespoon flour**
> **5 eggs, separated**
> **15 g/1/2 oz butter**
> **1 teaspoon ground nutmeg**
> **freshly ground black pepper**
> **2 tablespoons grated Parmesan cheese**

### mushroom filling

> **30 g/1 oz butter**
> **125 g/4 oz button mushrooms, sliced**
> **3 spring onions, chopped**
> **440 g/14 oz canned tomatoes, drained and mashed**
> **1 teaspoon chopped fresh oregano or 1/2 teaspoon dried oregano**
> **2 teaspoons chopped fresh basil or 1/2 teaspoon dried basil**
> **freshly ground black pepper**

## tip from the chef

*Eggs have always been a symbol of new life and prosperity. It is said that if you dream about eggs then the future will bring riches and good luck. However, beware if the eggs you dream about are broken or cracked, as this indicates you will quarrel with your lover.*

# creamy
## vanilla custards

■□□ | Cooking time: 10 minutes - Preparation time: 10 minutes

## method

1. To prepare strawberries, holding the stalk, dip each strawberry in chocolate to partially coat. Place on nonstick baking paper and allow chocolate to set at room temperature.
2. Place egg yolks and sugar in a bowl and beat for 2 minutes. Place cream in a saucepan and bring just to simmering, then remove from heat and slowly pour into egg mixture, while continuing to whisk vigorously. Stir in vanilla essence.
3. Transfer custard to a clean saucepan and cook over a low heat without boiling, stirring constantly for 5-10 minutes or until custard thickens. Remove from heat and set aside to cool slightly.
4. Spoon custard into individual serving glasses and allow to cool completely. Serve with chocolate strawberries.

...........
**Serves 4**

## ingredients

> **4 egg yolks**
> **1/3 cup/75 g/2 1/2 oz caster sugar**
> **1 1/2 cups/375 ml/ 12 fl oz double cream**
> **3 teaspoons vanilla essence**

### chocolate strawberries

> **250 g/8 oz strawberries**
> **100 g/3 1/2 oz dark chocolate, melted**

## tip from the chef

*Gentle cooking is essential for custard or it will curdle. To ensure success you may wish to place the bowl over a saucepan of simmering water rather than cooking it over a direct heat.*

# crème caramel

■□□ I Cooking time: 25 minutes - Preparation time: 10 minutes

## ingredients

> **4 eggs, lightly beaten**
> **1 teaspoon vanilla essence**
> **¼ cup/60 g/2 oz caster sugar**
> **½ cup/60 g/2 oz milk powder, sifted**
> **2 cups/500 ml/16 fl oz milk, scalded**

### toffee

> **½ cup/125 ml/4 fl oz water**
> **½ cup/125 g/4 oz sugar**

## method

1. To make toffee, place water and sugar in a small, heavy-based saucepan and cook over a low heat, stirring constantly until sugar dissolves. Bring to the boil and boil, without stirring, until light golden brown. Pour into 6 lightly greased ½ cup/ 125 ml/4 fl oz capacity ramekins.

2. Place eggs, vanilla essence, sugar and milk powder in a mixing bowl and beat until sugar dissolves. Whisk in milk, then pour into ramekins.

3. Place ramekins in a baking dish with enough boiling water to come halfway up sides of ramekins and bake at 180°C/350°F/Gas 4 for 20 minutes, or until a knife inserted into the center of custard comes out clean.

4. Remove ramekins from baking dish and set aside to cool. Chill before serving. To serve, invert chilled custards onto serving plates.

............
**Serves 6**

## tip from the chef

*To scald milk or cream, rinse a small heavy-based saucepan with cold water, add the milk or cream and bring almost to the boil over a low heat, stirring occasionally. Scalding will help prevent curdling during cooking.*

# apricot
## meringue

■□□ | Cooking time: 28 minutes - Preparation time: 5 minutes

## method

1. Blend or process apricot halves with brandy, vanilla, sugar and egg yolks until smooth, about 1 minute. Pour mixture into a greased 20 cm/8 in round ovenproof dish. Bake in a moderate oven for 8 minutes, remove from heat and set aside.

2. Beat egg whites and extra sugar with an electric mixer until soft peaks form. Carefully spread meringue over the precooked apricot base. Return to moderate oven and cook for a further 20 minutes.

## ingredients

> **3 cups canned apricot halves, drained**
> **2 tablespoons brandy**
> **2 teaspoons vanilla essence**
> **3 tablespoons caster sugar**
> **3 eggs, separated**
> **1/4 cup caster sugar, extra**

**Serves 4**

tip from the chef

*Egg whites at room temperature beat up more rapidly and have a better volume than those straight out of the refrigerator. Correctly beaten egg whites will increase by 7-8 times their original volume.*

# floating islands

■ ■ □ | Cooking time: 20 minutes - Preparation time: 20 minutes

## ingredients

> **6 eggs, separated**
> **1 cup/220 g/7 oz caster sugar**
> **3 cups/750 ml/1¹/4 pt milk**
> **4 teaspoons vanilla essence**

### toffee

> **1 cup/250 g/8 oz sugar**
> **¹/3 cup/90 ml/3 fl oz water**

## method

1. Place egg whites in a bowl and beat until soft peaks form. Gradually beat in half the caster sugar (a) and continue to beat until stiff peaks form. This will take 7-10 minutes.

2. Place milk and vanilla essence in a saucepan and bring to the boil, then reduce heat to simmering. Using 2 dessertspoons, shape spoonfuls of egg white mixture and poach in milk for 2 minutes (b). Using a slotted spoon, remove meringue and place on absorbent kitchen paper. Reserve milk.

3. Place egg yolks and remaining sugar in a large bowl and beat until thick and creamy. Gradually pour in reserved milk (c) and beat for 3 minutes longer. Transfer to a large saucepan and cook over a low heat, stirring constantly and taking care not to allow the mixture to boil, for 8-10 minutes or until custard thickens.

4. To make toffee, place sugar and water in a small saucepan and cook over a medium heat, stirring constantly until sugar dissolves. Continue to cook, without stirring, until golden. Remove from heat and set aside to stand until bubbles subside. Place meringues on a pool of custard. Spin toffee and use to decorate dessert.

## tip from the chef

*Also called snow eggs, this romantic dessert is an example of poached meringues. Custard and meringues can be made ahead of time and chilled, but toffee should be made and spun within an hour of serving.*

...........
**Serves 4**

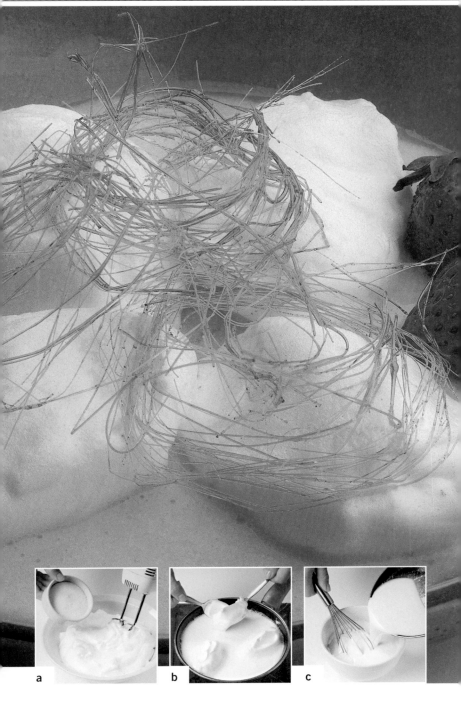

a

b

c

# blini
## and strawberries

■ ■ □ | Cooking time: 15 minutes - Preparation time: 15 minutes

## method

1. Place milk, sugar and yeast in a bowl and stand for 10 minutes or until frothy. Place egg yolks and sour cream in a bowl and whisk to combine. Stir in yeast. Whisk flour into yeast mixture, cover with a damp tea-towel and stand in a warm place for 1 hour.
2. Place egg whites in a bowl and beat until soft peaks form. Fold into yeast mixture.
3. Heat butter in a large frying pan and cook tablespoons of mixture for 1 minute each side or until golden. Set aside and keep warm.
4. To make sauce, place strawberries and Cointreau in a food processor or blender and process until smooth. Push through a sieve. Serve blini with fresh strawberries and strawberry sauce.

## ingredients

> 1 cup/250 ml/8 fl oz milk, warmed
> 1 teaspoon caster sugar
> 15 g/$^1$/$_2$ oz active dry yeast
> 3 eggs, separated
> $^1$/$_2$ cup/125 g/4 oz sour cream
> 1$^1$/$_4$ cups/155 g/5 oz flour, sifted
> 30 g/1 oz butter
> 250 g/8 oz strawberries, quartered

### strawberry sauce

> 250 g/8 oz strawberries
> 3 tablespoons Cointreau

...........
**Serves 4**

## tip from the chef

*Originally savory pancakes, blini are also delicious served with fruit, as in this recipe. You might also like to make them using different types of flour such as polenta, wholemeal or buckwheat flour. Each tastes a little different but all are wonderful whether served as a sweet or savory dish.*

# sabayón
## with berries

■ ■ ■ | Cooking time: 5 minutes - Preparation time: 5 minutes

### ingredients

> **3 egg yolks**
> **¼ cup/60 g/2 oz caster sugar**
> **2 tablespoons Cointreau**
> **1 teaspoon gelatin**
> **¼ cup/60 ml/2 fl oz white wine**
> **½ cup/125 ml/4 fl oz double cream, lightly whipped**
> **250 g/8 oz fresh berries of your choice**

### method

1. Place egg yolks, sugar and Cointreau in a bowl over a saucepan of boiling water. Cook, whisking constantly, for 3 minutes or until thick. Remove from heat and set aside.
2. Place gelatin and wine in a small bowl and dissolve over a saucepan of simmering water. Whisk into egg mixture and continue to whisk until cool.
3. Fold cream into mixture, spoon into serving glasses and chill. Serve with berries.

...........
**Serves 4**

### tip from the chef
*In this creamy version of the Italian dessert zabaglione the basic mix is enriched with cream and set with gelatin to make a delectable summer dessert.*

# liqueur strawberry soufflé

■☐☐ | Cooking time: 35 minutes - Preparation time: 10 minutes

## method

1. Place Amaretto, Grand Marnier and strawberries in a bowl and toss to combine. Set aside to macerate for 30 minutes.

2. Place egg yolks and sugar in a bowl and beat until thick and creamy then fold in flour. Combine milk and vanilla essence and whisk into egg mixture. Transfer to a saucepan and heat gently, stirring constantly, until custard boils and thickens. Reduce heat and simmer for 2 minutes. Set aside to cool slightly.

3. Place egg whites in a bowl and beat until stiff peaks form. Fold quickly and lightly into custard, using a metal spoon.

4. Place half the strawberries in the base of a well-greased 20 cm/8 in soufflé dish and pour over half the mixture. Repeat with remaining fruit and mixture.

5. Bake at 180°C/350°F/Gas 4 for 25-30 minutes or until well risen and golden brown. Sprinkle with icing sugar and serve immediately.

## ingredients

> 2 tablespoons Amaretto
> 2 tablespoons Grand Marnier
> 250 g/8 oz strawberries, sliced
> 4 egg yolks
> $1/3$ cup/75 g/$2^1/2$ oz caster sugar
> $1/3$ cup/45 g/$1^1/2$ oz flour
> $1^1/4$ cups/315 ml/ 10 fl oz milk, scalded
> $1/2$ teaspoon vanilla essence
> 5 egg whites
> icing sugar

...........
**Serves 6**

## tip from the chef

*Keep leftover yolks and whites in an airtight container in the refrigerator. Place 1 tablespoon of water over the yolks to prevent a skin forming. Yolks will keep for up to 3 days and whites for up to 10 days.*

# lemon
## soufflé omelette

■□□ I Cooking time: 5 minutes - Preparation time: 5 minutes

### ingredients

> **2 eggs, separated**
> **2 tablespoons cream**
> **4 tablespoons caster sugar**
> **1 tablespoon freshly squeezed lemon juice**
> **1 tablespoon freshly squeezed lime juice**
> **1 tablespoon butter**
> **icing sugar, for dusting**

### method

1. Using an electric mixer, beat egg yolks, cream, sugar, lemon juice and lime juice for 1 minute.
2. In a separate bowl, beat egg whites until soft peaks form. Fold egg yolk mixture into the whites, one tablespoon at a time.
3. Melt butter in a medium frying pan until sizzling. Pour mixture into pan, cook until golden underneath, about 1-2 minutes.
4. Transfer pan to grill and cook until top of omelette is dry to touch. Using a spatula, ease omelette onto serving plate, fold in half and dust with icing sugar. Serve with fresh cream and blueberries if desired.

**Makes 1**

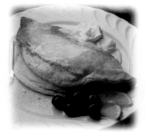

### tip from the chef

*For best results butter should be foaming, but not colored, when you add the egg mixture. This means that the omelette will begin to cook straight away.*

# index